Doggerland: The History of the Land that Once Connected Great Britain to Continental Europe

By Charles River Editors

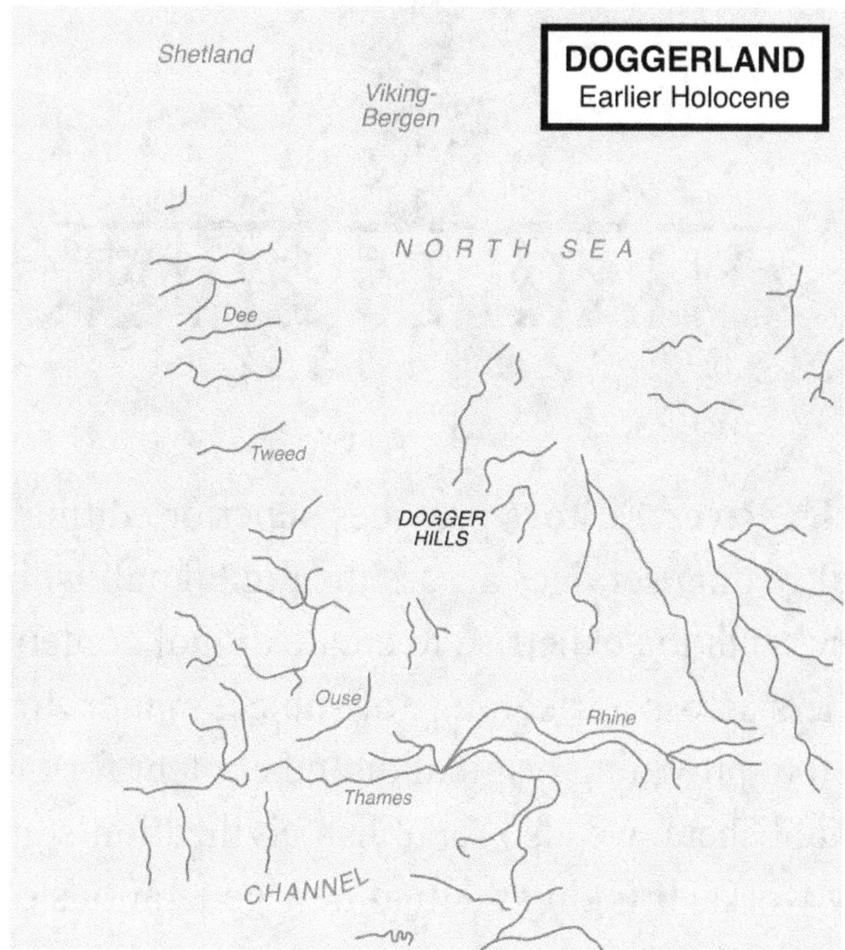

Max Naylor's map of prehistoric Doggerland

About Charles River Editors

Charles River Editors provides superior editing and original writing services across the digital publishing industry, with the expertise to create digital content for publishers across a vast range of subject matter. In addition to providing original digital content for third party publishers, we also republish civilization's greatest literary works, bringing them to new generations of readers via ebooks.

Sign up here to receive updates about free books as we publish them, and visit Our Kindle Author Page to browse today's free promotions and our most recently published Kindle titles.

Introduction

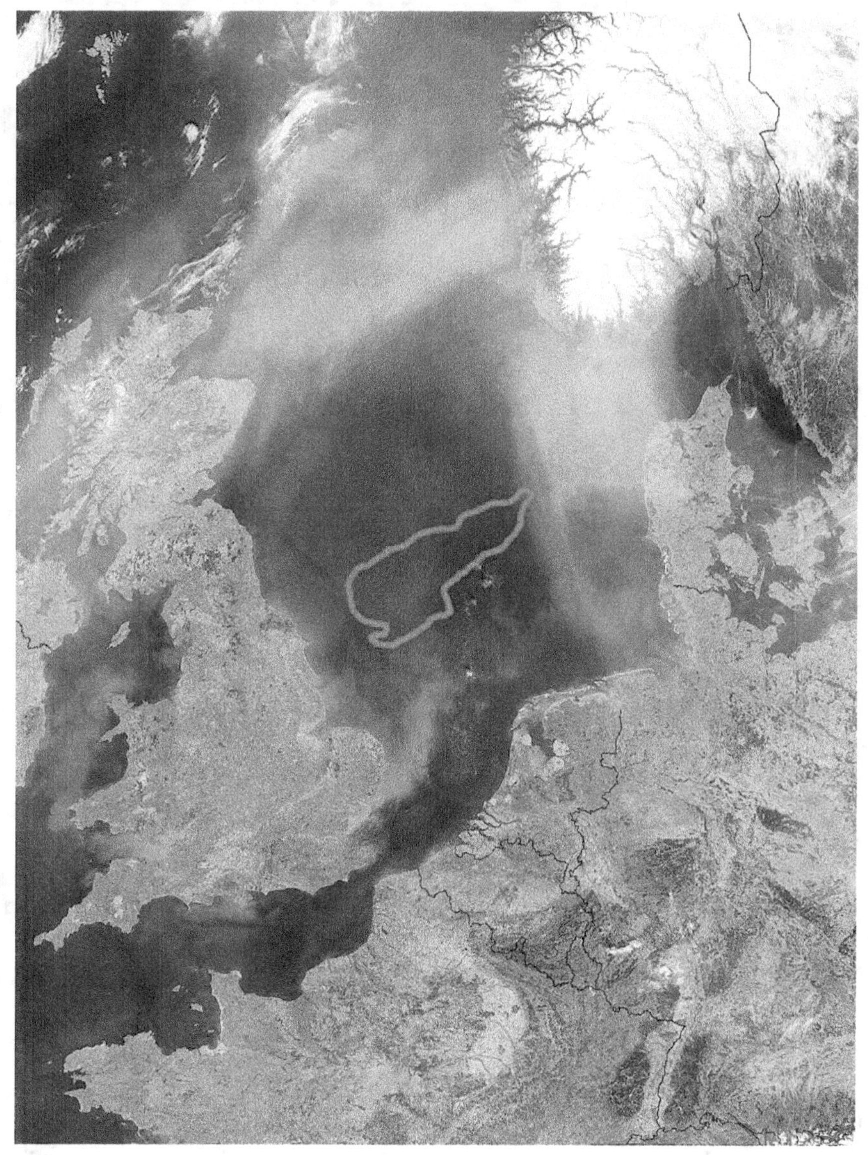

A satellite photo of the area today

The early history of Earth covers such vast stretches of time that years, centuries, and even millennia become virtually meaningless. Instead, paleontologists and scientists who study geochronology divide time into periods and eras.

The current view of science is that Earth is around 4.6 billion years old, but despite all of the scientific advances made in the past few centuries, including an enhanced understanding of Earth's geological past, relatively little is known about the planet's early history. That said, it is apparent that Earth has never experienced a static period in which the dynamism of oceans and land masses ceased to evolve, even if human perception of tectonic shifts cannot easily make note of epic topographical "adjustments" occurring over vast periods of time. Within the immediate range of people's senses, the history of important continental events assumes a point of scientific archival knowledge largely devoid of the visceral and experiential. The "slowness of the geological processes"[1] leads us to mistakenly assume that the Earth beneath our feet is stable, and that the bulk of subterranean events and their triggers, invisible beneath the surface of land or water, can be ignored.

Well beyond the breadth of human existence, major land masses have through the ages reformed into disparate configurations on an inevitable path toward apocalyptic continental collisions. Within that process, our present tectonic reality shows no sign of slowing. Speculation holds, for example, that the African continent will in time

---

[1] Magnet, Doggerland, the Europe once inhabited and today submerged in the waters of the North Sea - www.magnet.xataxa.com/en-diez-minutos/doggerland-la-europa-una-vez-habitada-y-hoy-submergida-en-las-aguas-del-mar-del-norte

overrun what is now the south of Europe. As an aid to perspective, population centers such as Venice and other iconic present-day cities are unlikely to survive what is to us an interminably lengthy natural process.

In the distant past, the continents were not so separate. The southern portion of the globe was at one time occupied by a "supercontinent" dubbed "Gondwana" or "Gondwanaland" that existed 600 million years ago. The mass included present-day South America, Africa, Arabia, Madagascar, India, Australia, and Antarctica. The term "supercontinent" was coined by Austrian geologist Eduard Suess, an expert on the Alps who helped lay the basis for the study of paleography and tectonics. The latter was to replace the "drifting continent" theory with "the study of the architecture of the earth's outer rocky shell."[2] In the late Paleozoic Age between 254 to 544 million years in the past, a global supercontinent commonly known as Pangea included the entire masses of Gondwana, Eurasia, and North America as the two northern continents collided.

Added to the shifting of continents away from what has been theorized as an original "supercontinent,"[3] other natural events have contributed to life's tenuous existence. The unexpected oceanic covering of dry land masses by

[2] Britannica, Eduard Suess, Austrian Geologist – www.britannica.com/biography/Eduard-Suess
[3] National Geographic Society, Continental Drift –
   www.nationalgeographicsociety.org/encyclopedia/continental-shift/

sudden seismically-driven tsunamis is more familiar to modern societies, and the sudden destruction wrought by these errant waves brought about by either volcanic action or sub-oceanic landslides is an ever-present danger to coastal communities. But equally perilous are slower alterations caused by climate change, a subject that has only recently begun to gain more attention.

On the other hand, the famed "lost city" of Atlantis has been a point of intense interest for thousands of years, and the notion of a submerged civilization is not uncommon. Inundated cities have remained a regular feature of the planet since people developed coastal enclaves a few thousand years ago. The early twentieth century theory of a floating land mass was in the decades following Suess' career eclipsed by the acceptance of tectonic plates and the effects of their relentless friction as one passes under another. Such ongoing action affects not only land masses, but the vast oceans in which they are situated. Relocation of water on a grand scale is common to geological annals as a dominant and dynamic majority element.

Among the most significant water displacement phenomena in the Western world was Doggerland on the northern European continent. The notable inundation occurred in both a steady and eruptive fashion covering a vast stretch of former tundra, a land bridge between today's British Isles and the European continent. The event brought about the modern English Channel and an expanded North Sea, and unlike the early supercontinents, the inundation of Doggerland took place after the appearance of people. Incrementally submerged since roughly 18,000 years ago as the climate warmed, the patch of sea between Britain and Europe is the subject of much recent scientific scrutiny. Several fields are participating in the inquiry as to how and why the inundation took place, and the nature of the peoples that settled there. This encompasses earliest man to Neanderthals and on through the Mesolithic prototype of the modern European.

The sunken plain that has commonly been dubbed Doggerland is based on its highest point, a now submerged island ridge called Dogger Bank. The name has been associated for several centuries with Dutch fishing vessels called Doggers. These two-masted craft fished the area for cod over hundreds of years. Where the island ridge once sat above the water as the last portion to be submerged, the prominent sand bank is now regarded as both a shipping hazard and treasure trove of potential research.

Doggerland: The History of the Land that Once Connected Great Britain to Continental Europe examines what the area was like, the processes that led to it being submerged, and ongoing studies of it. Along with pictures depicting important people, places, and events, you will learn about Doggerland like never before.

Doggerland: The History of the Land that Once Connected Great Britain to Continental Europe

About Charles River Editors

Introduction

The First Visitors

The Replacements

Submergence

Culture

The Past and Future of Doggerland

Online Resources

Further Reading

Free Books by Charles River Editors

Discounted Books by Charles River Editors

The First Visitors

The vast swath of the Northern Sea first appeared in a late nineteenth century work of H.G. Wells entitled *A Story of the Stone Age*. Considering that it was authored well before modern research was undertaken, Well's work is surprisingly accurate. The prehistoric setting is indeed a land bridge between Britain and Europe, and its description of a place with abundant resources was later confirmed as surprisingly close to the truth. Always eager to associate the Atlantean legends with scientific discovery, the literary world and press have often added a flourish to the Doggerland region such as "The Atlantis of Britain"[4] or "Prehistoric Garden of Eden."[5]

Of course, scientific descriptions of the lightly explored Doggerland are most trustworthy, with a reliance upon survey data provided by numerous oil companies seeking drilling sites in the North Sea. From the eastern and southeastern portions of the British coast to Scandinavian shores, the dimensions of the plain under survey encompass 18,000 square miles.

The first attempts at mapping the sea floor show a land of gently sloping hills, marshland, wooded valleys, and

---

[4] Alicia McDermott, Atlantis of Britain: Prehistoric Territory of Doggerland Prepares to Unveil Its Secrets, Ancient Origins, Sept. 2, 2015 – www.ancient-origins.net/news-history-archeaology/atlantis-britain-prehistoric-territory-doggerland-prepares-unveil-secrets-020510

[5] Alicia McDermott

swampy lagoons, leftover conditions from the Mesolithic Period, which lasted from c. 8000-2700 BCE. As important as the topographical picture of the ancient tundra was the discovery of river systems operating along the way before complete inundation. These were the progenitors of what became known as iconic modern rivers. However, in the Mesolithic phase, they were at best in an embryonic state winding throughout Doggerland with little topographical resistance. What is now the Elbe flowed into a large inland lake, later to join with the sea. The Rhine traveled across the northern swath of the continent from east to west until it reached Britain. There, it collided with what is now the Thames, flowing in the opposite direction.

The middle of three phases in the Stone Age, the Mesolithic is marked as an age of upgraded toolmaking and the transition from a hunter-gatherer's life to modern farming. At the height of its settlement period, thousands of families are estimated to have lived in Doggerland. At the greatest extent, 100,000 individuals are estimated to have inhabited the region, and they are often mentioned as being the potential inhabitants of Atlantis. However, Plato described Atlantis as being an advanced society destroyed by inundation through its own technological abuse.

Modern Europe's genetic ancestor was no such type of individual. Where mythical descriptions of Atlantis suggest a classic, clean city, the Doggerland region was primitive, harsh and sparsely settled. Only the requirement of an abundance of resources is fulfilled in any comparison.

In popular culture, the term Neanderthal is used as a colloquial insult for a degenerate or someone perceived as stupid. This seems to have been the case even from the first recognition of the Neanderthals as a species. The first Neanderthal fossil discovery was that of a child's skull in Belgium in 1829, but it was badly damaged. Another would be discovered in 1856 in a limestone mine of the Neanderthal region of what is present-day Germany, and a skull with differing distinct traits (indicating a different species than the Neanderthals) would be discovered just over a decade later in southwestern France. The latter specimen would come to be recognized as an example of the species *Homo Sapiens*, and these anatomically modern humans arrived in Europe between 45,000 and 43,000 years ago, around the time the Neanderthals are believed to started going extinct.

The Neanderthals are a member of the genus Homo just like *Homo sapiens* and share roughly 99.7% of their DNA with modern humans (Reynolds and Gallagher 2012). Both species even lived briefly during the same time in Eurasia. However, the Neanderthals evolved separately in

Europe, away from modern humans, who evolved in Africa.

Physically, the Neanderthal skeleton was much more robust, suggesting that there was more room for muscle attachment. However, while Neanderthals were stronger than modern humans, the average height of the Neanderthal male was shorter, standing at only about 5'5 tall.

Other physical characteristics that set the Neanderthals apart from modern humans were certain skull traits. The skull in general was low and elongated, featuring a sloping forehead with an occipital bun (a bone projection at the back of the skull), whereas modern humans have a more vertical forehead with no occipital bun. The cranial capacity of the Neanderthal skull was also greater than the modern human at 1,500–1,740 cc, and it lacked a chin and had more circular eye orbits, in contrast to *Homo sapiens*, which have a chin and tend to feature more rectangular eye orbits (Wolpoff 1999). Despite these differences, the Neanderthals may have been recognizable enough to interact with *Homo sapiens* or even blend in with *Homo sapiens* for the thousands of years they lived together in Europe.

The Neanderthals lived in Europe and Asia for nearly 200,000 years and thrived in these regions, but they went extinct between 40,000 and 30,000 years ago, around the same time that modern humans began arriving in Europe. This has prompted much speculation as to the nature of the interactions between Neanderthals and *Homo sapiens*, especially since some researchers believe they interacted with each other for over 5,000 years before the Neanderthals began going extinct at different times across Europe. One hypothesis is that *Homo sapiens* displaced the Neanderthals and were better suited for the environment, and it is obviously possible if not likely that these two groups had become competitors for food and other resources, with *Homo sapiens* being more successful in the end.

  If such close interactions were taking place, there is also a possibility that the relatively new-to-Europe *Homo sapiens* brought pathogens from Africa with them that were unknown to the Neanderthal's immune system. A more recent example of this type of resulting interaction is the European expansion into the Americas, which brought diseases like smallpox that the natives of America had never experienced before, especially diseases resulting from the domestication of animals. It is possible that the domestication of the dog by *Homo sapiens* may have contributed in spreading foreign diseases among the Neanderthals.

Whether or not this occurred, it is highly likely that the interactions between the two groups became much more intimate at one point. The Neanderthals were able to make and use a diverse set of sophisticated tools, control fire, make and wear clothing, and create decorations and ornaments. There is even evidence that the Neanderthal buried their dead with grave offerings, a practice that is also associated with later *Homo sapiens*, which suggests the two species were exchanging ideas such as tool making and rituals. Archaeological sites from Spain to Russia have been discovered that contain transitional stone tools associated with either *Homo sapiens* or Neanderthals. From the archaeological evidence alone, it is difficult to determine the level of interactions that were held at these sites. These sites may have been used at the same time.

There is also strong genetic evidence of mating between *Homo sapiens* and the Neanderthals. This theory was proposed as far back as 1907, but it was not until recently that science has been able to demonstrate that the genomes of all non-Africans include portions that are Neanderthal in origin. It is estimated that around 2% of the DNA in Europeans and some Asians is shared with ancient Neanderthal DNA. Ötzi the Iceman, who died about 5,300 years ago and is the oldest European mummy yet discovered, was found to have had an even higher percentage of Neanderthal DNA. Geneticists also discovered that while modern human nuclear DNA is linked with ancient Neanderthals, no mitochondrial DNA, which is passed on from the mother, is. This suggests that Neanderthal males were able to mate with *Homo sapien* females and produce fertile offspring that then carried the human mother's mitochondrial DNA, whereas the *Homo sapien* males who mated with Neanderthal females produced only sterile or unsuccessful offspring. Whatever the case may be, not much of the Neanderthal genome seems to have survived within the gene pool of modern humans today.

The Neanderthals and Mesolithic proto-Europeans must have made limited contact at the point where one disappeared and the other began to flourish. The earlier Paleolithic was the harsher of the two environments, but both were dangerous. The Neanderthals appeared in Doggerland around 40,000 BCE near the end of the last glacial age, and survived into 18,000 BCE, at which point the last thaw began. The most recent Ice Age had nearly run its course, allowing mammals to enter the region, and the appearance of humans in the area was largely dependent on megafauna migrations such as mammoth and rhinoceros.

Some call the time of the Neanderthal's entry onto the Doggerland tundra a "failed interglacial"[6] period, where the thawing of the glaciers was intermittent and reversible, a restive but erratic period between eons of glaciation. The early years saw great climatic instability, but at least mild enough to make access to Britain "practicable."[7] Still a severe, treeless environment not yet fully prepared for the modern human, it was nonetheless "well-stocked"[8] with large-body herbivores seeking the prairie grasses.

During the Neanderthals' tenure, dramatic swings of the interglacial period featured an initial phase of relative mildness. The second exhibited a long, slow deterioration of temperature, ending with a third phase of extreme cold. Similar to the recent Ice Age, pollen counts point to a low rate of vegetation growth due to both temperature and concentrated grazing, with reindeer herds added to the large game population. However, unlike the true Ice Age, no ground was frozen the year round during the thaw, and the precipitation rate stood at the present day's general mark.

In an archaeological debate as to the hardiness of the first Neanderthals, archaeologist Mark White discusses the various ways in which the new residents "buffered themselves by sophisticated cultural means."[9] Colleagues,

---

[6] Mark J. White, Things to Do in Doggerland When You're Dead: Surviving O1S3 at the Northwestern-most Fringe of Middle Paleolithic Europe, *World Archaeology*, Vol. 138 No. 4, Debate in "World Archaeology" Dec. 2006, pp547-575

[7] Mark J. White

[8] Mark J. White

[9] Mark J. White

however, questioned how even the Neanderthal was able to "tough it out"[10] in such an unforgiving environment. The general body shape of the early resident conformed to standard models for successful arctic adaptation. Overall, he enjoyed little "thermoregulatory"[11] advantage over his descendants on the continent, outside of a limited excess of subcutaneous fat, helpful for self-heating.

An abundance of hair was an asset, and all successful arctic creatures from the arctic fox to the mammoth were without exception "woolly."[12] Still, the Neanderthals put themselves under considerable stress, on most days living outside their "thermoneutral zone."[13] This made the balance of their lives "energy-expensive."[14] With the increased scarcity of grass, Neanderthals subsisted on a "hyper-carnivory"[15] diet of animal fat. Much of the Neanderthal calorie-burn went to traveling long distances in order to procure short term perishable necessities, such as wood for fires. Fire had long been a part of the Neanderthal arsenal for survival, but with such a lack of material on the barren plain, it was unlikely to be sustained as an ongoing regimen. Above all, they were required to follow the large animals, and forced to share whatever climate they were able to withstand. This meant

----

[10] Mark J. White
[11] Mark J. White
[12] Mark J. White
[13] Mark J. White
[14] Mark J. White
[15] Mark J. White

regular retreats into milder zones when the fauna so chose. There, they traveled in small, mobile groups. For the most severe northern climes, the Neanderthals were mostly visitors during the summer.

In time, the Neanderthals went extinct, and scientists are still uncertain as to the reason. To that point in history, they had followed successful "adaptive strategies"[16] through a number of glacial cycles. However, despite being "cold-adaptive,"[17] their use of rudimentary clothing may have eventually proved the fatal flaw as they moved too far north. For the Neanderthal travelers, there was a "clear geographical limit"[18] to northern movement, and Doggerland's "wind chill" may have caught them off guard. Equatorial climes do not share as wide a temperature range as do arctic regions, and the colder regions tend to be windier. Subjected to extreme conditions as a daily regimen, the Neanderthals lived a life of increasing "cold-stress"[19] and failed to solve its lethal effects by making the leap from "simple" to "complex" clothing. This strategy for survival required pre-adaptation, and the collective's in-the-moment strategy may have been a case of "too little, too late."

---

[16] Ian Gilligan, Neanderthal Extinction and Modern Human Behavior: The Role of Climate Change and Clothing, *World Archaeology*, Vol. 39 No. 4, Debates in "World Archaeology," Dec/ 3009. Pp499-514
[17] Ian Gilligan
[18] Ian Gilligan
[19] Ian Gilligan

The hypothesis that anatomically modern humans migrated out of Africa roughly 150,000 years ago and replaced the Neanderthals has led to much speculation over what exactly happened to the species. These theories tended to mirror the political attitudes of whichever period they were put forth in. For example, in the late 19th century, it was believed the superior modern human was able to conquer the brutish Neanderthals, reflecting the belief in the superiority of the European "race." In the 20th century, this idea was expounded on, positing that the Neanderthals were violently eradicated (reflecting the negative attitudes and dangers of world conflicts). More recently in the 21st century, the influence of global warming and environmental changes are taken into account, reflected in the theory that the Neanderthals went extinct because they could not deal with the end of the glacial period in Europe and elsewhere. Either way, the fact remains that the Neanderthals went extinct, and given the acceptance of the "out-of-Africa" hypothesis and revelations from genetic evidence, it seems unlikely the Neanderthals wholly evolved into modern humans.

The violence hypothesis was first put forth in the early 20th century after remains were uncovered for both early humans and Neanderthals that showed signs of possibly violent behaviors. Long bones, such as the bones of arms and legs, had been broken and healed together, resulting in generally non-linear bones. It cannot be stated with any amount of certainty that those injuries were caused by interspecies violence, but one recent find from Iraq, dating to between 50,000-75,000 years ago, indicates a Neanderthal was killed by a human. Shandir III, a 40–50 year old male, had injuries to one of his rib bones that were consistent with a projectile (Alper 2003). Since it is thought that Neanderthals did not possess projectiles, but rather used spears for thrusting, it would mean that *Homo sapiens* would have been responsible.

Of course, a single instance of interspecies violence is not nearly enough to prove the hypothesis that modern humans wiped out the Neanderthals, but it is evidence of interaction and the advantage that a projectile weapon had over the close combat thrusting spear used by the Neanderthals. This also would have been advantageous for hunting, and as the modern humans began moving in on the territory of the Neanderthals, they would have been competing for the same food sources. It is possible that the projectile weapons provided enough of an advantage to allow modern humans to dominate the landscape.

It is also during this period that the climate became warmer, so the big game the Neanderthals traditionally hunted became more sparse. The consumption of small game, such as rabbits, increased, and projectiles would have had a clear advantage in the hunting of small game.

Modern humans also brought with them another tool for hunting: domestic dogs. These dogs would have been able to assist in catching or flushing out small game, another distinct advantage.

Furthermore, the arrival of domestic dogs may have also brought pathogens that the Neanderthal immune system was not accustomed to fighting. While no direct evidence has yet been able to isolate specific zoonoses, or diseases that can be transmitted from animals to humans, there are plenty of examples in history that demonstrate what happens when isolated groups of people without domesticated animals meet groups with them. The Native Americans of North America and South America did not have a system of domestication like that of the Europeans, so when the Europeans first began interacting with the Native Americans, the natives' immune systems had to deal with new pathogens that were completely alien to the land. Smallpox would go on to wipe out a catastrophic number of natives across the Americas. That said, the spread of disease would have been slow for the Neanderthal population since they had isolated populations.

The climate shifted again in Europe during the Last Glacial Maximum. During this time, a Heinrich event took place as large portions of icebergs in the North Atlantic broke off and resulted in significant inputs of cold and fresh water to the ocean. This new intake of fresh and cold water altered the circulation patterns of the ocean, resulting in global climate fluctuations. The climate thus shifted to becoming increasingly cold, with the worst conditions coming approximately 24,000 years ago (Finlayson 2009). Food sources would have migrated from the colder climates, and there were likely fewer food sources to replace them.

The Neanderthals may not have been able to physically adapt either to the changing environment or to the physically different modern humans. The relatively low stature of the Neanderthals and the robust limb bones made moving across the landscape 8–12% more costly in terms of energy and calories required (Hora 2014), which would made it all the more difficult for Neanderthals who were chasing small game and competing for diminishing food resources.

Another important aspect to consider is the interbreeding between early humans and the Neanderthals. The Neanderthal Genome Project, which consists of a group of scientists sequencing the Neanderthal genome, have found evidence of interbreeding between early humans and the Neanderthals, with modern humans of European or Asian descent sharing around 1-4% of their DNA with the Neanderthals. It is thought that this interbreeding took place between 50,000 and 60,000 years ago (Brahic

2014), and some scientists have placed the interbreeding as far back as 100,000 years ago. That would mean modern humans not from Africa were more closely related to the Neanderthals than they were to the humans who remained in Africa.

Another non-exclusive hypothesis for the demise of the Neanderthals comes from the Campanian Ignimbrite eruption. Occurring around 39,000 years ago, this volcanic eruption near Naples, Italy spewed volcanic ash into the sky, which would have caused a big enough shift in the weather to affect vegetation. Findings from the Mezmaiskaya Cave show a rapid reduction of plant pollen, suggesting that the plant life may have rapidly died out during this time (Than 2010). This would have led to a decrease in the main food source for the plant-eating big game animals that the Neanderthals hunted.

Evidence of Neanderthals suffering from nutritional issues during this period verifies that they were struggling to live during that time. Fossil evidence shows that animal remains from this period were more processed than those of animal remains from other periods; these remains were more highly fragmented and featured a significant amount of hammer stone marks from the Neanderthals trying to crack them open. The small bones of the feet from animals, for example, were also cracked open in order to extract marrow (Hodgkins et al. 2016).

This volcanic eruption naturally would have affected modern humans as well, but they had a much greater population size, which meant that even if a large portion of them died out, there still would have been enough survivors to continue the population and survive on the available food sources. Furthermore, there were more early humans in Africa who could migrate into Europe later.

It is even possible that the cognitive abilities of the Neanderthals also played a role in the extinction of the species. Early humans were developing forms of art in cave paintings and figures, and they had already developed new forms of hunting available game, while the Neanderthals were relatively slower in the development of stone tools and show fewer signs of art or abstract thinking (other than supernatural beliefs). This view roughly reflects the early 20th century view held by Boule that the "superior" early man was the reason for the extinction of the Neanderthals. The more recent way of phrasing this has been that the Neanderthals were driven to extinction by the invasion of behaviorally modern *Homo sapiens* (Sterelny 2012: 62). Put another way, the superior language skills, the superior capacity to convey information, and the superior ability to innovate may have helped *Homo sapiens* contribute to the extinction of the Neanderthals.

In all likelihood it was probably a combination of environmental factors, the inability to adapt to new conditions, the competition for resources with the migrating modern humans, and the occasional conflict and interbreeding with *Homo sapiens* that collectively contributed to the disappearance of modern man's genetic cousin. Either way, it meant that a new species of human would populate Doggerland.

The Replacements

The last Neanderthal migrations gave way to the somewhat milder Mesolithic winter. Some pre-historians grant the period a less conservative and slightly earlier span of dates in northwestern Europe, the height occurring between 10000 and 4000 BCE. The designation of Mesolithic was introduced into the archaeological world in the mid-nineteenth century by Hodder Westropp, who added it to John Lubbock's prominent work entitled *Pre-historic Times*. Westropp wrote and published what was likely the first handbook on archaeology. Among principal features of his new designation was a marked departure from "chipping" tools of the Old Stone Age to a "polished" type employing a wider variety of materials and accessories, characteristic of Mesolithic use.

In the final period of glaciation, northern Europe remained bound by ice. As the glaciers began to warm, a broad continental shelf became exposed between Britain and Scandinavia. With the surplus of melted water, the seas began to flood the lowlands at a rapid rate, geologically speaking. Hastening the eventual devastation of the shelf was the rupture of an ice dam across the way in the young North American land mass centered around eastern Canada, and the upper U.S. Lake Agassiz was named for the first scientist who figured out its origins and function in one of Doggerland's most destructive moments. The lake was the largest freshwater body of water in the world, and at one point contained more than all others combined. Held back by the Laurentide Ice Sheet, it ran for 1,500 kilometers and averaged just over 200 feet in depth. It was the ice sheet that caused the trouble by retreating and readvancing continually. The Laurentide sheet adjusted itself in one instance to the point at which the lake rivaled the state of California. Blocking the eastern outlet before opening again, the sudden release from the swollen water level raced across the Atlantic with Doggerland directly in its path. Estimates of immediate water rise on the northern European plain was prodigious, and estimates still may be conservative. Some set the European rise at an instantaneous one to three meters in 11,000 BCE.

Human life was present on the northern continent to experience the climate of this period. The descendants of

Ice Age peoples, the Mesolithic human nevertheless differed greatly from the Neanderthal. As the proto-European arrived in Doggerland, the genetic group was broken into two origins. Haploid U bore the common genetic makeup of the Paleolithic and may have begun its migration from the Balkans. The rare Haploid K group is thought to have originated in the Middle East.

During the years of abundance on the plains of Doggerland, the challenge facing the proto-European was much the same as it had been for the Neanderthal. However, solutions were available as survival technology was enhanced through time. The first signs of a critical shift in human history were seen in this age, where innovation extended past enhanced tools and weapons. During this time, a transition ensued from the "hunter-gatherer" model of nomadic living to stationary farming settlements. Rudimentary farming and the first signs of animal domestication appeared in their earliest forms. To the south, embryonic cities were taking root in a faster-paced, warmer environment.

The Mesolithic hunter-gather had arrived thousands of years earlier as the animals reappeared during the glacial thaw. The climate eased somewhat for human habitation, enabling forests to be added to the landscape. This change was to the benefit of most, but not all, as important grasses diminished. The Mesolithic family was not required to travel such distances for wood, as forests increased its variety and abundance. Honing skills that are still valued today, the Mesolithic human doubtlessly considered his relation to nature as a "fundamental element"[20] out of necessity. Despite present-day society's increasing distance from such a concept, we have begun to regain an appreciation for the "bushcraft"[21] of our Mesolithic ancestors. It is shown in both the universal pastime of "camping," and by our revived interest in "green" living. Like modern humans, the Mesolithic experienced grey and hungry days, and dark and bright nights. Unlike most of twenty-first century residents, they were unlikely to throw away a fully functional artifact for the instant gratification of a new "model."

Northern Europe was among the last post-glacial regions of the planet to be settled due to the erratic climate. Where much of the final thaw followed a smoother process around most of the world, the early European population was initially forced to wait through erratic changes that forestalled the milder conditions. Chief among them was a period referred to as the *Younger Dryas*. A time of disruption in the warming trend that lasted from c.12,900 to 11,600 BCE, it developed over the space of 100 years, and lasted 1,300. The *Younger Dryas* took its name from

---

[20] Caroline Wickham-Jones, Living in Mesolithic Scotland, Archaeology –
www.mesolithic.co.uk/blog/2019/07/03/3052-2/
[21] Caroline Wickham-Jones

the *Dryas octopetala*, a small yellow wildflower of the rose family, typical of vegetation in a cold and open arctic environment.

A subsequent period known as the *Preboreal* predominated from 8,350 to 7,050 BCE, and for northern Europe, marked the beginning of the sub-designation of the Holocene period, a warming trend that first appeared in Greenland. Its predominant feature was the emergence of large vegetation. As before, human presence in Doggerland was not primarily responsive to changes in climate, but rather to animal migration. The post-arctic animal kingdom was driven by a greater sensitivity to climate change than that possessed by the newly-arrived humans. For the Mesolithic migration, progress was further hindered by more than climatic instability as in the previous eras, but by a prodigious Baltic Ice Lake that prevented plant and animal movement to the north.

The proto-Europeans spread relatively quickly throughout northern Europe, following the ebb and flow of animal migrations, settling then retreating during periods of cold snaps. The Baltic Ice Lake, however, was not the only deterrent to widespread settlement. As the "zones" of Doggerland are viewed today, the coasts of Britain, France, and Belgium make up the western portion. Central Doggerland includes shorelines of Germany, Denmark, and the Netherlands. Most of

Scandinavia, Estonia, Latvia, the northern regions of
Poland, and Russia make up the eastern portion.

In France, the Paris Basin included the Seine, Somme,
and Loire river drainages. The rate of settlement there was
sporadic at best, and foragers seldom ventured far above
the Seine due to the extended severe conditions and a
generally slow glacial recovery. Experiencing fewer
disruptions, the Paris Basin remained a gradual process by
comparison, but the cold was extreme. To the north and
east, sudden climate reversals brought severe drops in
megafauna numbers, especially mammoths that had
originated in Russian Doggerland to the east, not to return
until the latter years of the Mesolithic age.

In Britain, the preponderance of evidence for settlement
comes from recovered tools and other artifacts from the
sea floor, currently under analysis by British
archaeological institutions. Similar sites have appeared on
the seacoasts off the Netherlands and Belgium.
Unfortunately, they cannot yet tell us where each settler
group originated, or the nature of their intended
destinations. Bordering the North Sea Basin in general,
coastal settlements suggest several retreats and
recolonizations. A number of settlements that remain in
Schleswig-Holstein of northern Germany show a similar
trait, appearing to represent an eastern expansion of
settlers moving across a continental land bridge to Britain.

Denmark's first examples of settlement were found through evidence of animal butchery, predominantly reindeer.

Determining a precise migratory chronology is a daunting task, as have been attempts at underwater surveys. Different regions of Doggerland pose different challenges. Some projects are inter-professional, complicated by such inconsistencies as dating systems used by archaeologists and marine surveyors. An abbreviated form of archival dating before the year 2000 AD is fifty years older than the radiocarbon dating system employed through 1950.

Results from disparate chronometric systems produced a certain degree of mistrust among the non-scientific public who perceived the entire pursuit of historic dating as a flawed process. Adding to the confusion were the varied oceanic conditions found through Doggerland's extremes. The area of present-day Finland was the final portion of Europe to deglaciate. The Norwegian Channel featured a westward moving advance of the Fennoscandian Glacier, slowing the infusion process of fresh and brackish water. In the search for human artifacts and other clues to the Mesolithic daily regimen, science had to take care to recognize which phase of development was providing their discoveries.

With the mandate to pull up stakes and depart at certain times, the settlers in question fulfilled the first phase of discovery. However, their sporadic presence in relation to the changing climate placed them in the pioneering phase, not truly as settlers in a permanent sense. They had not yet mastered their destination, and to classify new artifacts could not be tied to permanent settlements.

The first examples of Mesolithic artifacts under the North Sea were brought up from the ocean floor by fishermen trawling the region. Discoveries first came to light by way of "beam trawling," the dragging of heavy nets along the seabed. Naturally, everything on the ocean floor came up as well. Crewmen manning the nets were shocked at what they found, but since such items were of no value to their profession, most examples were cast back into the depths. Eventually, archaeologists caught wind of the discoveries, and requested that fishermen keep them up to date, and to bring bones and artifacts to shore.

In 1931, scientists came into possession of a harpoon tip fashioned from bone and extending nearly nine inches. It was retrieved from the sea bottom by the trawler *Colinda* within a lump of peat and the artifact was inscribed with elaborate decorations. Items of barbed antler and human bone were to become a distinguishing feature of the Mesolithic settler, a far cry from the rudimentary Neanderthal tool. The piece was found 25 miles off the

British coast and dating placed it at a point between 10000 and 4000 BCE.

Accompanying artifacts included textile fragments and canoe paddles for a craft of more than 30 feet in length. A similar Mesolithic site was discovered near the coast of Denmark, and included sunken floors, canoes, fish traps, and burials within the riverbed of the ancient Rhine. In an exception to the Mesolithic community, a Neanderthal skull fragment 40,000 years of age was brought up with numerous artifacts 30,000 years younger.

At first, no one wanted to believe the age and description of what was appearing in the nets. Other items passed along by the trawlers included bones and tools surpassing 9,000 years in age. Occasionally, a large tusk or other sizeable animal part appeared. With them came mammoth teeth and portions of extinct animals such as the bull-like Auroch, making denial more difficult.

**A picture of a woolly mammoth skull found in the
North Sea**

Near the end of the twentieth century, amateur
paleontologist Dick Mol persuaded a ship's captain to
bring the bones to him, and to make careful notes of
coordinates where each item was found. The Dutch
researcher is a lifelong specialist in mammoths and
ancient breeds of rhinoceros and is affiliated with several
museums. The dutiful fishing captain presented Mol with
an entire well-preserved human jawbone with worn
molars in 1983. The example was radiocarbon dated at
9,500 years and is believed to have come from a burial
site where it had "lain undisturbed"[22] for that duration. A

---

[22] Laura Spinney, Searching for Doggerland, National Geographic –
www.naturalgeographic.com/magazine/2012/12/doggerland/

second prize was brought up some years later in the form of a stone axe with a decorative zig-zag pattern. It is surmised by investigators that such plentiful sites must have been situated near a river current, where congregated families lived on the banks. Mammals presumably gathered there, and fish were likely available.

In the early decades of the twenty-first century, specialty ships from the U.K. were outfitted with elaborate mapping and artifact analysis technologies to "systematically examine"[23] the Doggerland sea floor. Most of the work was done in the vicinity around Brown Bank, also known as Brown Ridge. This location lies between Britain and the Netherlands, offering scientists a shoal of 30 kilometers to scrutinize. While analyzing the sediment layers, a concentration of plants and animals was taken from the bottom, including wild cattle and pigs, reindeer, and other mammals.

Heading the survey was Vince Gaffney of Bradford University. Gaffney and the Bradford program have digitally reconstructed nearly 18,000 miles of the area, roughly the same size as the Netherlands. At Bradford University's IBM Visual and Spatial Technology Center, the team is now able to project images of Doggerland at a new level of accuracy.

---

[23] DW, Doggerland: How did the Atlantis of the North Sea Sink? – www.dw.com/en/doggerland-how-did-the-atlantis-of-the-north-sea-sink/a-55960379

These were published in the first decade of the twenty-first century, arousing the interest of fellow institutions. The artifacts recovered from the sea floor can be viewed up close as archaeologists are no longer hindered by the massive task of retrieval. A number of artifacts was put on display at the British Royal Society's Summer Science Exhibition of 2012 in London.

In the search for settlements, scientists have not reached the point where one can say "x marks the spot or 'Joe created this,'"[24] but clear outlines of communal work have been located through unnatural manipulation of the soil. The presence of mounds surrounded by ditches and fossilized tree stumps on the sea floor suggest an intent to establish a more permanent home.

Other scientific teams explored and excavated more shallow water sites of the Mesolithic in and around a Danish island in the Baltic Sea. The results revealed a "surprisingly advanced"[25] Mesolithic fishing culture, complete with ornately decorated canoe paddles and long thin canoes. Similar excavations have been undertaken at Wismar Bay on the German Baltic coast under Harald Lübke of The Centre of Baltic and Scandinavian Archaeology of Schleswig, Germany. Lübke documents the point at which Doggerland residents shifted their diet

---

[24] CBS News, Doggerland, Northern Europe's own lost city of Atlantis discovered off Scotland, July3, 2012 – www.cbsnews.com/doggerlandnorthern-europes-own-lost-city-of-atlantis-discovered-off-scotland/
[25] DW, Doggerland

from freshwater to marine fish as the sea level rose.

Research has been conducted in Goldcliff at the Severn Estuary of Wales. Martin Bell of the University of Reading excavated the area for over two decades, probing the mud flats near an ordinary ridge that formed the edge of an island. After blasting the muddy soil with a high-pressure hose, Bell discovered 39 sets of footprints made by three or four individuals heading in opposite directions. Several camps of up to 10 people were placed in the time period in which they would have witnessed visible sea rise and the death of the salinized forest beaten down by the general conditions. Some light was shed on communal activities of the settlements as the study marked the likelihood of mass annual gatherings and various other social events.

Submergence

At the height of Mesolithic culture in Doggerland, the sea was rising at a rate of three to six feet per century. In East Anglia, six feet of rising tide shifted the coastline by several kilometers. In the lower plain region, inland lakes became estuaries. Outer Silver Pit, east of Flamborough Head, is a valley running in an easterly direction near Dogger Bank from Britain. The floor produced massive sandbars which would have posed extreme dangers for log boats of the time attempting to reach British shores.

Ethnographic literature of similar hunter-gatherer societies such as the northern Inuit were consulted in the statistical progression of response to sea rise. As with the Mesolithic settler, the sea was at first a boon to civilization, but its rapid takeover rendered standard knowledge useless. The tribal territory was contorted to the point where the collective lost its ability to read the seasons and recognition of river behavior eroded. Presumably, civilizations were in time cut off from ancestral hunting, fishing, and burial grounds. With no understanding of how far the rising sea would go, a settlement had no way to calculate what distance would ensure escape.

Multiple population displacements seem inevitable under such a circumstance, and settlements exist along Britain's eastern cliffs that show the remains of dwellings rebuilt several times. Huts were found dating from the seventh century BCE. The settlers' inland movement eventually brought them into unfamiliar and hostile competition with rival communities as they escaped the lowland, but little change was noted in the physical designs as settlements were reestablished.

In time, all life was forced to higher ground. Doggerland went on to exist as a series of islands where refuge was available for a time, but inevitably the only escape was to the shores of Britain, central Europe, and Scandinavia.

The eventual coastline of the northern continent came to rest at a distance of approximately 300 kilometers from end to end, or 186 miles following what came to be known as the Storegga tsunami.

Making the gradual transition to higher ground in every part of Doggerland must have appeared more than sufficient in consistent time periods, but societies that knew nothing of seismic events were in for a tragic surprise. Eventually, only the highest patches of Doggerland remained above water, as the only remaining island shrank to the size of Wales, approximately 23,000 square kilometers. At that point, relentless albeit gradual climate change gave way to a major event.

The fiercest arguments have been waged for decades over whether the Norwegian Storegga tsunami was the coup de grâce for the last portion remaining above water. The suboceanic landslides that delivered an all-encompassing devastation to Europe's former lowland plain 8,200 years ago was by any account "apocalyptic."[26] To assume that the last remaining fragment of the small patch of island remaining would never be able to stand up to such punishment is understandable, but some among the scientific community have remained unconvinced.

As had the Neanderthal, the Mesolithic inhabitants were

---

[26] DW

bound to experience their share of seismic catastrophes, while climate change worked slowly to alter the environment in between. Long after the Agassiz spill over, around 8,000 years ago, a series of seismic events far below the surface of the Norwegian coast created a series of lethal tsunamis that swept over the whole of northern Europe once again. A towering series of waves caromed from east to west across the remaining region of Doggerland. In advance of these events, the rich megafauna of the region began to die off from the loss of grass and proliferation of forestland from the warming trend. In time, all life was forced to higher ground. More rapid migrations escaped successfully, but permanent settlements on the island is open to question.

The Storegga tsunami still tends to be historically perceived as one colossal event. However, multiple landslides caused the occurrence, constituting a series of assaults with surface-borne inundation as its visible centerpiece. For studies relating to our own relationship with land and oceanic environments, understanding the accurate tsunami process of Storegga and other catastrophes is essential. Researchers estimate that at a distance stretching 290 kilometers, 3,500 cubic kilometers of rock and debris plunged into the North Sea at the Norwegian end of Doggerland.

Estimates vary as to the height of the subsequent waves

that swallowed the region. Some set the number at 20 meters, and others estimate a much higher figure depending on the location of impact. In the Shetland Islands north of Scotland, the 20-meter calculation conforms to the sedimentary data, while in other locations the estimations are considered somewhat conservative. Regardless, Storegga was of sufficient force to alter the landscape of Britain 40 kilometers inland. The Imperial College, on the other hand, cites other locations receiving waves only 16 feet in height, perhaps suggesting that Britain bore the worst of it as the target destination.

For many years, scientists have assumed that the Storegga tsunami created Dogger Bank, an obstacle course of sand bars now menacing the shipping industry. However, Gaffney and the Bradford team, in the lead for the most comprehensive investigations of all, claim that the tsunami did not in the end destroy the island, and that the northern part of Doggerland might have survived by slowing the force of the impact with its hills and forest.

Of the original land above water, only marshes were left. People and animals certainly perished, and the location of organic remains suggests that multiple inundations overcame the bulk of the island temporarily. It is the most recent conclusion of the Bradford surveys that 700 years after the Storegga event, the sea level again rose through climate change, this time covering the last of Doggerland entirely.

Despite the magnitude of Storegga, an event not to be seen in the region again, other forces were clearly at work. Following exhaustive analysis of the Storegga effect, the event appears to have been a lethal shock to a pre-existing pattern gradually unfolding over a span of 20,000 years. Such a time period is not long in geological terms, and Doggerland appears to have continued to exist above water as an archipelago of islands for several centuries following the last of the Storegga tsunamis. They, too, succumbed to climate change as well. According to the avenues of science with which humans are familiar in the present age, it is difficult to produce an alternative to the climate change theory.

Rising sea waters borne of climate change have forced populations to move since the first appearance of humans, and some underestimated the severity of their situation and failed to escape. Before the inundation that caused today's configuration of the North Sea, Doggerland has been described as a likely "paradise"[27] for the ancient hunter-gatherers, and as the collection of artifacts grows, the estimation of human numbers residing in or traveling through northern Europe has grown considerably.

Subsequent surveys have altered the calculation of sea

---

[27] Smithsonian Magazine

rise to a greater magnitude than previously thought. This engaged the human community of Doggerland in "a delicate minuet"[28] with the encroaching ocean, with ramifications they were ill-suited to understand or predict. They responded with good basic logic, but for a lesser catastrophe. As familiar landmarks disappeared with each generation, explorers, pioneers, and settlers simply packed up and headed for higher ground. Had the Mesolithic human honed an instinct for the way nature moves suddenly in glacial regions, they could have otherwise prepared for 3,000 years of erratic climate. Warming and cooling, the retreat of the ancient Pleistocene glaciers, rapid sea rise, extinction of the essential megafauna, and the emergence of forestland all came with some advance notice.

These conditions could be outrun, but the arrival of Storegga, however, ran contrary to the notion of gradual adaptation. Mesolithic people's lack of preparation rivals that of modern times, where the catastrophic event equation remains the same. In any discussion of seismic events that pose threats to modern society, people today share the localized and sporadic occurrences of such phenomena with people who lived during the Mesolithic. However, when climate change becomes relevant to the question of sea levels and global temperatures, scientists

---

[28] Smithsonian Magazine

are discussing a larger planetary issue that leaves no one unaffected.

With a body of research gathered in "a major undertaking,"[29] the geological world feels comfortably certain that although the Storegga tsunami dealt a crippling blow to northern Europe, it did not cause the demise of the land mass. A tsunami, like any lesser wave, gains momentum, reaches its impact point with land, breaks, then subsides. Such was the case with Doggerland, and resettlement was possible. However, no defense existed or exists now against a general warming of the atmosphere after a glacial thaw, save reduction of agents that speed up the warming process. Mesolithic culture possessed no polluting industries with modern emissions, and the land still succumbed. The lack of human participation makes the apparent reality more dire, as modern humans play a greater role in their warming cycle. However, the absence of Mesolithic industry also demonstrates how the alternating pattern of glaciation and thaw is a central rhythm to the planet's climatic personality, and Doggerland seems to have suffered from being in the wrong place at the wrong time, surrounded by ice dams, glacial ranges, and inland lakes during a post-glacial melt.

---

[29] Smithsonian Magazine, *Never Heard of Doggerland? Blame Climate Change from Millenia Ago* – www.smithsonian.com/science-nature/never-heard-of-doggerland-blame-climate-change-from-millenia-ago-72154423/

Culture

As surveys continue to follow settlers to the outer edges of the new coastline, hazelnuts, acorns, and nettles became important parts of the Mesolithic diet, suggesting that the presence of large-bodied animals was less reliable than in the past. These nuts and large leafy plants gave way to the addition of corn and wheat as the nomad took his first steps in land management and subsequent ownership.

Swamps were intentionally burned, with trees felled for dwellings by chipped and polished tools. Stone harpoons, fishhooks and arrowheads are still found in abundance and traps have been uncovered within the river and stream systems. The discovery of rudimentary log boats and canoes has increased and among the most surprising revelations of recent years are early attempts at artificial roads, wooden trackways by which to safely cross areas of marshland.

The larger communities have been uniformly found nearer the current coastlines, while the earlier internal settlements are smaller and fewer. Once at the outer edges of the new land formations, previously unfamiliar groups made contact. Evidence persists of exchanges between disparate traditions of raw materials and finished tools. DNA studies suggest that with the more widespread movement of the general population, intermarriage became increasingly common across Eurasia. The entirety of Europe's genetic makeup, including residual Neanderthal elements, can be found in the region, and serves as a basis for a varied ancestry in modern Europe.

As with the more distant prehistoric collectives, an art culture formed within the Mesolithic. Whether the period's paintings carry a religious or spiritual urge is unknown. One might suggest that such depictions existed as a means of social communication, record-keeping, examples of male bravado, or simply for a sense of personal satisfaction. Using whatever was available, Mesolithic art tends to exhibit a small range of color predominated by red ochre and patterns are starkly geometric. Decorated artifacts include painted pebbles, ground stone beads, pierced shells and teeth, and amber. Items uncovered at the site of Star Carr to the north of Yorkshire include red deer headdresses. From this, the most important Mesolithic site in Britain dating from 9,000 BCE, enormous troves of artifacts have been drawn from waterlogged peat since the mid-twentieth century.

In addition to the increasingly sophisticated crafts and artworks, the first small cemeteries of Mesolithic communities in Doggerland have been uncovered, the largest located in Skateholm, Sweden. To date, 65 internments have been located. A few are inhumations, while others are cremations and some contain highly ritualized "skull nests."[30]

A funerary feature of the Neolithic is the "special treatment"[31] of the human head. The crania, mandible and jaw are often employed as "grave goods," and are at times inserted on stakes in shallow pools. Interpretations of this practice are speculative, but some suggest an overt display of territoriality. Other archaeologists suggest that "social stratification"[32] could be at work, in a hierarchy built on prestige.

In some examples, the specimen appears related to large-scale acts of violence. In general, hunter-gatherer communities exhibited a lower propensity for violence than either herders or horticulturalists. Although signs of violence can be seen in some skull nests, they are considered objects of decoration. With the rise in social pressure, alien groups collided in a smaller space along the coastlines and farmers vied for land ownership, an alien concept to the hunter-gatherer. Competition for resources became a new social problem as families left the plains. In such conditions, the violence rate gained parity between the community types. Among the typical "grave goods" were various tools and jewelry, shells, and animal

[30]Kris K. Hirst, Mesolithic Period, Hunter-Gatherer-Fishers in Europe, Thoughtco., Feb. 24, 2019 – www.thoughtco.com/mesolithic-life-in-europe-before-farming-171668

[31] Rick J. Schulting, Mesolithic "skull cults," Research Gate, University of Oxford – www.researchgate.net/publication/275542043_Mesolithic_%27skull_cults%27

[32] Thought.co

and human figurines. In the latter Mesolithic, graves were constructed with large stone blocks in the style of mausoleums, houses for the dead.

   With the space shrinking between human collectives, Mesolithic hunters began an early arms race with new types of hunting projectiles. In this way, climate change ushered in an age of territorialism that has never left the human species. New shapes for spear tips and arrowheads included the triangle, crescent, leaf-shaped, trapeze, and mistletoe monoliths. Drought exacerbated the competition for survival, in addition to erosion and wildfire, a going concern in the twenty-first century as well. The barbed point "projectiles" show signs of having been sharpened many times.

   A particular set of "tip" weapons uncovered were subjected to mass spectroscopy and collagen peptide mass fingerprinting. Spectroscopy studies an object's absorption and emission of light, and the dispersion into its component colors. Collagen peptide mass fingerprinting reveals biomarkers for species identification. The results were a shock to investigators because out of the four examples, two were human, the other two deer. Scientists are uncertain as to the use of human bone, guessing that it may carry a yet unknown cultural cause.

Advanced analysis of DNA has entered the inquiry in a way it could not only a few decades earlier. Scientists of the School of Life Sciences of Warwick University have made multiple breakthroughs in their study of sediment cores. The concept of biogenic mass, low-molecular products made of or by life forms essential to good health, changed along with events. Here, the field of archaeobotany has joined the inquiry. In the transition from a high animal fat diet to a regimen of plant foods paralleling the move to early farming, the first clues have come from present-day Poland. At the Calowanie site, core samples of plant remains were found to be interlaced with biogenic sediments that suggest the use of tubers and roots. This is the first example of a plant-based regimen, other than the ingestion of hazelnuts and chestnuts.

The samples made repetitive reference to woody trees as new ways of authenticating DNA developed. Antiquated methods were limited for probing damaged objects held under the sea for lengthy periods. Once unable to gather enough information on specific species, a new metagenomic assessment methodology assisted the process by scrutinizing the damaged ends of DNA molecules collectively instead of separately. We are thus able to ascertain whether an object has moved over time. A recent innovation has refined algorithms to define regions of "dark phylogenetic space,"[33] a visual hypothesis of an organism's history based on its relationships to a similarly evolving organism group.

Gaffney, working with the School of Archeological and Forensic Sciences at Bradford, declares that untangling a holistic picture of the Mesolithic legacy in Doggerland is "one of the last great archaeological challenges in Europe."[34] His important comparisons to the trajectory of modern events, especially in coastal areas, continue to grow an attentive public audience. In his most recent voyage, an 11-day expedition through the region was unique among previous efforts. Still using oil company maps, he admits that the Doggerland sea floor has been surveyed based on these charts "countless times."[35] However, this inquiry was intended to prioritize lost settlements. Although Brown Bank has produced thousands of samples already, it remains the most fertile target. With a new array of sensitive technologies, this trek has discovered fossilized forests and samples of compressed peat indicating marshland, the optimum environment for settlements. Where the artifacts dredged up were once fishhooks and spear tips, we have moved on to analyze pollen and insects as well.

---

[33] PHYS.org, Ancient DNA from Doggerland, separates the U.K. from Europe – www.phys.org/news/2020-07-ancient-dna-doggerland-uk-europe.html

[34] PHYS. org

[35] Natasha Ishak, Scientists on Verge of Finding Real-Life Atlantis Beneath the North Sea, All That's Interesting, August 6, 2019 – www.allthatsinteresting.com/doggerland

With surveys employing an enhanced technology, researchers such as Robin Allaby working at Warwick claim that the sea floor preserves DNA "extremely well"[36] if the desired object can be reached and extracted. Thus, it is now possible to reconstruct paleoenvironments for thousands of years longer than would be possible on land at the same latitude.

For Gaffney's latest twenty-first century voyage, the funding to illuminate the Doggerland sea floor was more forthcoming than it has ever been. He received 2.5 million Euro in an Advanced Research Grant from the European Research Council. Sophistication of technology keeps pace as greater areas of the continental shelf are made available to archaeologists. New data is accessible that was never pursued until the advent of novel modes of mapping, "DNA extraction and computer modeling."[37] Multi-dimensional models are being generated that demonstrate how Doggerland was colonized and lost, down to the individual organism.

The support is forthcoming in part from the increasing urgency to assert some control over our own environmental conditions. Catastrophic events are more likely to occur when the environment warms. Studying shocks to the world system such as those of Lake Agassiz

---

[36] Alice McDermott
[37] Alice McDermott

and Storegga, whether their involvement in Doggerland's demise was whole or partial, is a "comparative phenomenon"[38] to our immediate well-being.

Recent events are frightening enough, but do not generally compare with the Mesolithic disasters. Archaeologists have struggled to this point to define natural catastrophes, and archaeology of natural disasters is a much-needed emerging field. In the typical seismic emergency, other studies are preoccupied with immediate loss of life and destruction rather than long-term impact. In order to meet with the megaevents to come, present-day society must put in a more informed effort to cope with and adapt to prevailing changes.

Those driving the quest for ancient explanations with a modern sense of urgency are armed with new survey and excavation capabilities. However, a complicated set of actions and reactions found in Storegga render the process elusive, even after all the centuries that have passed. A recent entry into the field in support of Gaffney's inquiry is the Exeter Project headed by Byron T. Coles.

Exeter intends to make use of recent exploration to not only reconstruct Doggerland's landscape under the North Sea, but to "explore its cultural interpretations."[39] Three

---

[38] Cambridge University Press, A Great Wave: The Storegga Tsunami the end of Doggerland?, Dec. 1, 2020 – www.cambridge.org/core/journals/antiquity/article/great-wave-the-storegga-tsunami-and-the-end-of-doggerland/CB2E132445086D868BF508041CC1B827

primary papers authored by Professor Coles have been published dealing with a speculative survey providing greater access for archaeologists. The mission is a broad one, entailing advancements in bog bodies, sacred sites, wetland archaeology, shifting coastline cultures, coastal and estuarine environments, sedimentology, geomorphology, and geoarchaeology. It is Cole's hope that his efforts will soon lead to a new level of completeness in the survey of undersea sites.

The various projects in play are propelled forward by cooperative alliances between Britain and continental organizations. Archaeologists working for Vattenfall, a Swedish energy group developing wind farms offshore from Norfolk, have recovered unique evidence of the British side of Doggerland. This includes a unique set of core samples from the development survey, the most complete and extensive ever taken from the southwestern portion of the North Sea. They shed light on the environment in which the Mesolithic population lived, and how quickly they were required to adapt to the flooding that created the English Channel. According to Dr. Claire Mellet, Wessex Archaeology's Principal Marine geoarchaeologist, the samples cover a period of around 3,500 years.

---

[39] Cole, Byron, Archaeology, *The Doggerland Project*, University of Exeter –
www.humanities.exeter.ac.uk/archaeology/research/projects/title_89282_en.html

Other surveys of the area capture brief periods of time with isolated discoveries, while the Vatterfall effort provides a "continuous record"[40] of prehistoric changes before and during the time of flooding. This encompasses an area of 85 square kilometers. The successful project led to the scheduling of a more complete analysis in the following year, collaborating with Historic England, by way of Dr. Christopher Pater, Head of Marine Planning.

The importance of the Norfolk coast extending out a significant distance has been bolstered by the discovery of a Bronze Age Timber Circle at the Beach of Holme near Hunstanton. Gaffney has calculated the monument as standing below the highest water level experienced by the region, and dates to approximately 2,000 years before the "common era." Since farming was introduced around 4000 BCE, it likely represents two thousand years of "retreat"[41] in the face of encroaching seas since the monument was built. Gaffney believes that the land must have been vast. Following discoveries in the subsequent decades, he opines that as challenging as the process might be, we have now come to a stage where one can indicate where settlement was to occur, and "being able to do something about it. It's a world first."[42]

---

[40] Wessex Archaeology, The Secrets of Doggerland – www.wessexarch.co.uk/news/secrets-doggerland

[41] Bishop, Chris, Deep Sea Research off Norfolk Sheds New Light on Our Ancestors, Eastern Daily Press, Dec. 1, 2020 – www.edp24.co.uk/news/doggerland-may-have-survived-with-sea-tsunami-65751138

[42] Eastern Daily Press

The layman may wonder at the fuss extended over the dating of the tsunamis and other events, but to the scientist it is crucially important. Finding an answer to either pre-inundation, inundation by the tsunami itself, or a lingering survival following the event says much about pre-modern European history.

In the period following Dogger Bank's disappearance, science has redubbed the location Dogger Littoral. Numerous core samples have been taken from this specific piece of seabed that still sits higher than anything else around it. The questions challenging investigators in terms of westward travel can be answered more easily at the top of this former island.

If the hunter-gatherer on his way to becoming a farmer on its slopes did not disappear after all, they may have served as a cultural buffer between the Linear Pottery Culture and other emerging societies present a thousand years after Storegga, and the new coastlines.

The Doggerland Littoral may have been the meeting point and crucible for a rapid uptick in the tempo of societal development. The balance of the final transition to farming may have been tipped in this small region, with all the attending innovations and inevitable social tensions that pervaded the subsequent ages. Gaffney's new evidence clearly demonstrated the island's relevance to the transition and offers compelling proof that the island summit and its people survived the tsunami.

In the Brown Bank core samples, broken shells and other debris moved around by the tsunami were strewn throughout the lower level of the island. However, samples from the upper portion showed none of this material. New data from vibracore samples of ancient river systems drove home the point. Vibracore is a technique for high-quality sediment collection allowing deep penetration in a single deployment. As a contrast to drilling, coring, or auguring, it can be employed in a wide range of depths with less sample disturbance. The procedure worked equally well in the Outer Dowsing Deep, a marine trough off the coast of Lincolnshire.

Showing a high degree of turbation, the reworking of soil and sediments by animals and plants, the accelerated deposits were all confirmed by mutually supportive fields of sedimentology, paleobotany, and sedaDNA, genetic material taken from sediment. All dating is contemporary with Storegga. The summit of Dogger Bank was apparently not inundated by Storegga after all. For all its apparent destruction, the event may best be categorized as a "near miss" for the contemporary Doggerland farmers.

Former Mesolithic nomads may have been forced from this area to the coastlines of what is now Britain, but to characterize them as escapees would be inaccurate. Gaffney's later expeditions have paid off in determining some of the migration patterns. Mapping suggests that parts of Brown Bank, now 50 kilometers off the British coast, were elevated over 30 kilometers in the Mesolithic and overlooked an ancient river. Using chemical signatures, Gaffney realized that living the nomadic lifestyle didn't come as easily to the residents as it once had. Communities made a concerted effort to stay in one spot, changing their diet from land animals to fish instead of seeking out new scenery and hunting grounds. The body of DNA Gaffney gathered was prolific, suggesting an abundance of bears, boars, birds, spiders and mosquitoes, hazel and linden trees, along with the customary meadow grasses.

  In the central and eastern zones of Doggerland's edges, a new support group has arisen for finding and collecting artifacts. These citizens from various walks of life require no other credentials than to be a vigilant beachcomber. Long after the Mesolithic world was lost, a startling variety of relics began to wash up on the North Sea beaches in the Netherlands. In 2013, in the Dutch town of Monster, Willy van Wingerden, employed as a nurse, found her first mammoth tooth on the sand. Since that day, she has added more than 500 artifacts from the windswept beach known as Zandmotor, or "Sand Engine."

The finds were primarily Mesolithic, but not exclusively. Van Wingerden found an assortment of Neanderthal tools of river cobble, fishhooks, and human remains thousands of years old. She can nearly always rely on finding something on a given day. For scientists, one informative prize came from a tar-covered tool sitting at the water's edge. The Zandmotor enjoys special protection, having been set aside as a 70 million Euro experimental coast protection measure, allowing archaeologists to roam within an area of 21 million cubic meters of Stone Age material.

Unable to find these items in their submerged state, the impressive collection amassed from amateur researchers is a scientific feast. As it has been explained by researchers, the stretch of water off the Zandmotor is "not a blank area, it's not a land bridge,"[43] but one of the best spots in Doggerland for Mesolithic hunter-gatherers. The artifacts are found in shallow water, or in the sand with no apparent logic attached to the search, in a more suitable condition for DNA dating.

As interest among the local citizens increased, a home gathering was held for all beach searchers, with the directive for each to bring one or more artifacts that might

---

43 Andrew Curry, Lost world revealed by human, Neanderthal relics washed up on North Sea beaches, Science, Jan.30, 2020 – www.sciencemag.org/news/2020/01/relics-washed-beaches-reveal-lost-world-beneath-north-sea

interest the inquiry. In one day, 50 human skeletal fragments were assembled at the gathering. The flint flake with a gob of tar on one end, a 50,000-year-old handle, was a star of the event. The Neanderthal use of birch bark pressed to make tar was a revelation. On the Zandmotor, one searcher exclaimed that "There are complete cemeteries sucked up and sprayed on the beaches."[44]

Other discoveries stretching back to more distant dates confirmed that the broad northern swath of the European continent was also occupied by *Homo antecessor*, the early human thought by most to be a genetic dead end. Specific artifacts found by the amateurs are now being analyzed at the Max Planck Institute for the Science of Human History. These include teeth up to 10,000 years old, and intact DNA from five human individuals. The scientists, grateful as they are for the army of beachcombers, feel an urgency to move on to locating literal sites, so that maps can be created. At present, however, most are found accidentally.

In analyzing the true effects wrought by the Storegga event, Gaffney is quick to caution against understatement. He suggests that although the destruction may not have resulted in a complete inundation, there was much immediate devastation - "If you were standing on the shoreline that day, 8,200 years ago…it would have been a

---

[44] Andrew Curry

bad day for you."[45] In a transition to a more permanent settlement, the Mesolithic resident unwittingly brought much trouble on himself by taking a stand and adapting his diet rather than moving on. The island could have been a semi-permanent home provided the available resources were abundant. The migration would have understood that a lifestyle on the move was by comparison "short, brutish, and nasty."[46]

Farming eventually won out, and one can only wonder how effective the new way of life might have been on a rapidly shrinking acreage. In a study of a Mesolithic site along Britain's Bouldner Cliff off the coast of the Isle of Wight south of Southampton and Portsmouth, the diversity and points of origin among the developing Mesolithic community was well demonstrated.

The former assumption that southern Europeans experienced no connection with northern pioneers has been debunked. In a Mesolithic paleosol, former soil buried under sediment or volcanic deposits dated at 8,000 years in the past, one core of sealed sediments revealed much. Micro-geomorphology, studying the processes of micro-functions in the natural world, and ancient sedimentary DNA were used to reconstruct changes in flora and fauna in the settlements before the inundation.

[45] Guardian, Study finds indications of life on Doggerland after devastating tsunami – www.theguardian.com/uk-news/2020/dec/01/evidence-life-on-doggerland-after-devastating-tsunami-study
[46] Guardian

Results suggested a mix of oak forest with poplar, apple, and a variety of beech trees, along with a few herbaceous plants.

Cereals that could not have originated in the northern zone demonstrated contact with the south, already well into the process of grain farming. Farmed wheat in particular was found dating 2,000 years earlier than any such crop found in mainland Britain, and 400 years earlier than that of proximate European cities. The presence of these foods implies a functioning system of "sophisticated social networks"[47] from the south. Oliver Smith of the University of Copenhagen revealed DNA links between the southern and northern Mesolithic peoples, confirming not only cultural exchange but intermarriage.

Since Bouldner Cliff is located on the southernmost tip of Britain, no real barriers existed to the spread of farming products from the Balkan region to Doggerland's Atlantic zone. The spread of farming techniques to the northerners was likely swift. Southern Britain must have provided the contact points for the south and north, a probability receiving little consideration until recent years. The exchanges would not have been conducted on a civilization-wide scale. Still, the presence of southern items, however sparse, affirm that a well-developed Mesolithic people of south and southwestern Europe

---

[47] Guardian

consciously met "the advancing Neolithic front"[48] from the north. Following such contact, the hunter-gatherer replaced parts of his diet with a variety of corn, wheat, and barley. No one is certain whether the former hunter-gatherers met their fellow civilizations as newly arrived farmers, or whether they gradually transitioned to an agricultural way of life through southern instruction.

The Past and Future of Doggerland

Even in the scientific world, toying with a connection to Plato's Atlantis seems inevitable, whether in support or in debunking the association. Such is the case with Doggerland, where a line of questioning persists in returning to the comparison. However, much of the research is a direct confrontation to Plato himself.

Were Plato's descriptions to either be disproven beyond the shadow of a doubt, or confirmed to exist in a specific location, the case might be otherwise. However, as two unsolved mysteries, Atlantis and Doggerland cannot for now live apart. Atlantis has been characterized as the true heart of an ancient classic and enlightened world, while Doggerland merits attention as the true heart of Europe, geologically and culturally. The two entities are bound, accurately or not, as a progenitor of today's great Atlantic

---

[48] Smith, Oliver, Momber, Gary, Bates, Richard, Garwood, Paul, Fitch, Simon, Pallen, Mark, Gaffney, Vincent, Allaby, Robin G., Sedimentary DNA from a submerged site reveals wheat in the British Isles 8000 years ago, *Science New Series,* Vol. 347, No. 6225 (Feb.,2015 pp998-1001

continent filled with iconic and unique societies.

Robert Graves, "renowned poet and mythologist,"[49] considered the possibility of Atlantis and Doggerland being one and the same, but in time changed his mind due to inconsistencies in distance within his data. Eventually, he moved on to a hypothesis on the northern African continent. Rachael Carson, author of *Silent Spring*, was likely the first to cite Dogger Bank as Atlantean in her earlier 1951 book, *The Sea Around Us*. Somewhat later, Scandinavian writer Nils Olof Bergquist published his *Ymdogat-Atlantis*.

Frenchman Jean Deruelle has written much on the subject, as has Sylvain Tristan and Guy Gervis, the latter authoring two papers. British journalist Rob Waugh offered a modern illustrated article placing Atlantis at the bottom of the North Sea while touching on some recent discoveries. Other researchers, quasi-researchers, and popular writers merged Doggerland with dry lands to the north presently known as Viking-Bergen Banks, and promptly dubbed the combination as Atlantean. In 2012, the *BBCE Focus Magazine* conflated the Minoan Hypothesis with the North Sea, as Minoan artifacts had been found there. Whether they were native to Doggerland or brought there by a variety of individuals is unknown. Nevertheless, the highly-regarded BBCE

---

[49] Atlantipedia, Robert Graves, Doggerland, July 22, 2010 – www.atlantipedia.ie/samples/tag/robeert-graves/

claimed that their theory was the only archaeological hypothesis with "any serious claim on the myth."[50]

Robert John Langdon, author of *Prehistoric Britain: The Stonehenge Enigma*, claims that Mesolithic society entered Doggerland from North Africa, escaped inundation to Britain, and built Stonehenge as a memorial. He suggests that the Altar Stone of Stonehenge points directly to Doggerland as the location of Atlantis, adding that the Slaughter Stone, situated midway through the monument's structure, represents the flooded world.

Of the group, Deruelle tends to be taken with the most seriousness. His exhaustive Atlantean research includes a book that supports Doggerland as Plato's choice location in *L. Atlantides de mégalithes*. Despite its thoroughness and tantalizing case for an Atlantean connection, Deruelle's surprisingly well-considered effort met with scant attention. Location of the "Great Plain" is always a chief barrier to Atlantean research. Deruelle, an engineer and geologist, offered the best case yet. It was met by detractors and devotees alike as "rational [and] highly precise."[51]

In his reliance on Plato's word, however, Deruelle and his colleagues were cast into a dilemma. Plato sets the

---

[50] Atlantipedia

[51] Q-Mag-org, The Great Plain of Atlantis – Was it Doggerland? – www.q-mag-org/the-great-plain-of-atlantis-was-it-in-doggerland.html

Atlantean era at approximately 9,700 BCE, but simultaneously claims that the Atlantean government was engaged in a war of aggression with both Athens and Egypt. Neither of those states existed during that period. Thus, if one takes Plato's description of the war to heart, one must dismiss the date. If the war is given credence, his entire historical statement falls apart.

Supportive dating seems to favor the chronological portion of Plato's description. The philosopher offers detailed measurements as well that seem dubious at first glance. However, by including considerations not factored into most chronologies, Deruelle claims to make sense of them. Plato's topographical description begins by describing Atlantis as being of "flat and uniform level."[52] This is known to be accurate for Doggerland. All the way from the Netherlands, the ground of the sea floor rises "only by a hair's breadth every kilometer."[53] Most of that land was inhospitable, covered with ice sheets, and surrounded with 3,000-meter-thick glaciers over Norwegian mountains, with another atop the mountains of Scotland. However, the plain between barely undulates.

Another snag hit the Plato hypothesis in one single requirement: in order to be Atlantis, the land had to be dry in the years between 7000 and 3000 BCE. The answer

____

[52] Q-Mag-org.
[53] Q-Mg-org.

was discouraging, for Dogger Bank was already submerged by 6000 BCE. However, where others threw up their hands, Deruelle and his team produced new charts, with curved averages measuring all the oceans of the globe. Uniform and world-wide variations among sea levels, known by the term "eustatics," revealed a previous oversight, that the levels of shoreline around the world differ from measurements of sea level because the shoreline rises with the tide and falls when it subsides.

Deruelle claims as well that a mass of repressed volcanic magma formed in a bubble off the coast, a "compensatory bulge"[54] that elevated the earth's crust. Thus, since 18000 BCE, the beginning of the final thaw, ice has created a reverse effect. The ground was going up in Scandinavia but down around the location of the bulge. Deruelle concludes that a good portion of the North Sea may have been much higher, and subsequently much dryer. Plato's Atlantean description appears to have survived another round of questioning.

The comparison continues in Plato's claim that Atlantis grew two entire crop rotations per year. This rate of production seems unlikely for Doggerland's latitude. The Plato mania has reached a point at which theorists will stop at nothing to contort the Greek's descriptions into geologic and chronological reality, one way or another.

---

[54] Q-Mag-org.

Deruelle's work represents only a small portion of the laborious effort to match Plato's Atlantis with Doggerland. The technologically outfitted projects surveying the sea floor may respond to such literary-based inquiries as scientifically insufficient, but exploration of Doggerland has not heard the last of evidence on Plato's behalf.

Ancient Greece is not the only school of thought referenced by modern investigation of Doggerland and Atlantis. Historians have urged investigators to consult fourth century CE historian Ammianus Marcellinus, who relied on a lost work authored by Timagenes about 500 years earlier. The claim is made that the civilization of Gaus migrated from the Doggerland region, specifically from "distant lands and islands beyond the Rhine,"[55] the very center of Deruelle's Atlantean search under the North Sea.

Deruelle has theorized, as have others, that an individual among the Mesolithic migration may have at some point attempted the Dutch defense against water incursion, a system of dikes with which to resist the rising ocean. A hypothetical and enterprising chief could have possibly succeeded with such a notion, as three dykes protecting sides of the Doggerland Bank would have created enough open space to qualify it as a "great plain." However, it is

---

[55] Q-Mag-org.

calculated that such barriers would eventually be required to reach a height of 50 feet.

Many people today are of the prevailing opinion that manipulating the environment is possible, where it was once not. The caution to heed ancient history has manifested itself in a present-day European proposal to reclaim the sunken territory. This is to be accomplished through an allied effort in the construction of dikes and pumping stations.

Considering the expertise that sustains the land in the Netherlands every day, the idea of taking back the territories of the North Sea is not technologically ludicrous. Despite centuries of inundation, parts of existing Europe have been reliably reclaimed. Lands recovered through northern European engineering includes swathes of Holland, East Anglia, Frisia, Flanders and Jutland, all formed in this manner. Dykes have been dug to both stop and relocate the influx of water, while sea beds have been dredged to accommodate the depth of the general region. Support exists for the reclaiming of Happisburgh in Norfolk, and the island of Sylt. Others believe that the entire land mass can be retrieved.

As to the resistance, the claim is made that by right, these sunken lands belong to Doggerland and the North Sea, not to the Netherlands, United Kingdom, Belgium,

Germany, or Denmark. However, to award ownership to a body of water that simply flowed where it was allowed to flow is a romantic notion, and any patriotic bent toward a people who no longer exist as a community is baffling. No modern human is self-described as a Doggerlander in terms of nationality, as the DNA of the ancient settlers is now infused into modern Europeans. Physically, ethically, and politically, no such nation exists, except in the shared genetic heritage of present-day European states.

Other concerns, however, come to the fore with greater seriousness. Detractors of the proposal caution that if wholesale patches or the complete dimensions of inundated territory are restored as dry land, commerce will be stalled. The Baltic Sea will become a giant interior lake, much as it once was, halting all water trade across northern Europe. Seaports such as Liverpool, London, and Rotterdam will suffer economically, and a great increase in overland shipping will be required. Furthermore, the gulf current will risk interruption, creating a far harsher climate for parts of Germany and Poland. Issues with rivers will abound as estuaries long since lost may return in part. The entire project would require rechanneling streams that may collide with any number of modern entities, none of which existed in the Mesolithic Period.

Political considerations will surround dimensions of ownership from country to country. All northern

European countries are presently members of the European Union and individualism versus the larger alliance is certain to create friction. Britain, however, a major player in the Doggerland inundation, has left the European Union and could by some political machination or other be made the odd man out.

Untold billions in expenses would be guaranteed, and worse, the entire network of reclamation must be maintained. Europe would carry the burden of this necessity at the same time in which the thaw cycle is being repeated, precisely as it was thousands of years ago. How the myriad of minute to massive alterations would affect the lives of both humans and animals currently in place is not entirely known. With these unanswered questions, many might ask whether the dream of a larger Europe is a futile proposition, a northern pipe dream for geologic and economic expansion.

The geological implications of the broad historical Doggerland saga represent one of the longest archival searches for development of the European continent and citizen. It maps not only the ice ages and inter-glacial eras, but the arrival of the *Homo antecessors*, the Neanderthals, the Mesolithic hunter-gatherers, and their descendants, the present-day Europeans. For earlier societies, the only hope of survival was to flee, while the latter claims to possess a solution to the peril of the middle period of the Stone Age.

The signs for the present century are legion in this informative submerged land. However, we are well-equipped with solutions, should we choose to embrace them. Placing ourselves within the framework of the ancient process and calculating our own timetable is not beyond the powers of modern knowledge. The primary issues of the twenty-first century are not unfamiliar ones, and no reason exists for a state of perplexity. Among the chief differences between the ancient and modern culture is that the Mesolithic human was "flexible and mobile,"[56] where modern man is not. The number of present-day humans inhabiting the earth is far greater than in ancient times, and modern resources are more finite in terms of availability to demand. Modern economies have invested so heavily in a world currency structure and profit-generating corporate dance between producer and purchaser that many are too miserly to save their own lives. Generally non-nomadic, the twenty-first century is additionally invested in physical structures owned by the populace, and enterprises housed in immobile corporate temples assembled in the world's largest cities.

Modern society's own resistance to accepting the

---

[56] The Conversation, Doggerland's lost world shows melting glaciers have drowned lands before, and may again, May 9, 2014 – www.theconversation.com/doggerlands-lost-world-shows-melting-glaciers-have-drowned-lands-before-and-may-again-26772

scientific evidence of the last glacial thaw through the fate of Mesolithic people is a barrier to avoiding a similar tragedy. If unanimity of belief can be achieved, the war over spending whatever is necessary will commence within and between nations. That would likely be followed by assembling an international spirit of cooperation, not a simple feat in the twenty-first century.

Perhaps the most daunting task of all is to forge an understanding among modern humans that we are not separate from the evolution that passed through *Homo antecessor* and the Neanderthals. Despite the advances in technology, people are still at the mercy of planetary climate rhythms, intermittent catastrophic events, and a chronologically broad alteration of the planet's climate. What remains to be revealed in Doggerland's submerged lands under the North Sea designates the region as one of the planet's most useful laboratories in the process.

Online Resources

Other books about ancient history by Charles River Editors

Other books about Doggerland on Amazon

Further Reading

Atlantipedia, Robert Graves, Doggerland, July 22, 2010 – www.atlantipedia.ie/samples/tag/robeert-graves

Bishop, Chris, Deep Sea Research off Norfolk Sheds New Light on Our Ancestors, Eastern Daily Press, Dec. 1, 2020 – www.edp24.co.uk/news/doggerland-may-have-survived-with-sea-tsunami-65751138

Cambridge University Press, A Great Wave: The Storegga Tsunami the end of Doggerland?, Dec. 1, 2020 – www.cambridge.org/core/journals/antiquity/article/great-wave-the-storegga-tsunami-and-the-end-of-doggerland/CB2E132445086D868BF508041CC1B827

CBS News, Doggerland, Northern Europe's own lost city of Atlantis discovered off Scotland, July3, 2012 – www.cbsnews.com/doggerlandnorthern-europes-own-lost-city-of-atlantis-discovered-off-scotland/

Cole, Byron, Archaeology, The Doggerland Project, University of Exeter – www.humanities.exeter.ac.uk/archaeology/research/projects/title_89282_en.html

Curry, Andrew, Lost world revealed by human, Neanderthal relics washed up on North Sea beaches, Science, Jan.30, 2020 – www.sciencemag.org/news/2020/01/relics-washed-beaches-reveal-lost-world-beneath-north-sea

DW, Doggerland: How did the Atlantis of the North Sea Sink? – www.dw.com/en/doggerland-how-did-the-atlantis-of-the-north-sea-sink/a-55960379

Encyclopedia Britannica, Mesolithic – www.britannica.com/event/misolithic

Gilligan, Ian, Neanderthal Extinction and Modern Human Behavior: The Role of Climate Change and Clothing, Vol. 39 No. 4, *Debates in "World Archaeology,"* Dec/ 2009 pp499-514

Guardian, Study finds indications of life on Doggerland after devastating tsunami – www.theguardian.com/uk-news/2020/dec/01/evidence-life-on-doggerland-after-devastating-tsunami-study

Heritage Daily, Doggerland – Europe's Lost Land – www.heritagedaily.com/2020/05/doggerland-europe's-lost-land

Hirst, K. Kris, Mesolithic Period, Hunter-Gatherer-Fishers in Europe, Thoughtco., Feb. 24, 2019 – www.thoughtco.com/mesolithic-life-in-europe-before-farming-171668

Infobae, Doggerland: a land submerged in the sea that searches for the DNA of human history, July1, 2016 – www.infoebae.com/tendencias/2016/07/01/doggerland-una-tierra-sumergida-en-la-mar-que-busca-el-adn-de-la-historia-de-lahuminidad/

Ishak, Natasha, Scientists on Verge of Finding Real-Life Atlantis Beneath the North Sea, All That's Interesting, August 6, 2019 – www.allthatsinteresting.com/doggerland

Kubiak-Martens, Lucyna – Evidence for possible use of plant foods in Paleolithic and Mesolithic diet from the site of Calowanie in the central part of the Polish plain, *Vegetation History and Archaeobotany*, Vol. 5 No. ½ (1996) pp 33-38

Log Doggerland, Reclaiming Doggerland, A Hypothetical Landscape, Oct. 21, 2010 – www.log.doggerland.net/2010/10/21/a-hypothetical-landscape/

Magnet, Doggerland, the Europe once inhabited and today submerged in the waters of the North Sea – www.magnet.xataxa.com/en-diez-minutos/doggerland-la-europa-una-vez-habitada-y-hoy-submergida-en-las-aguas-del-mar-del-norte

McDermott, Alicia, Atlantis of Britain: Prehistoric Territory of Doggerland Prepares to Unveil Its Secrets, Ancient Origins, Sept. 2, 2015 – www.ancient-origins.net/news-history-archeaology/atlantis-britain-prehistoric-territory-doggerland-prepares-unveil-secrets-020510

McDermott, Alicia, Scientists find evidence for tsunami

that washed out Doggerland, *Ancient Origins*, July 17, 2020

McGreevy, Nora, Smithsonian, Smart News, Study Rewrites History of Ancient Land Bridge Between Britain and Europe, Smithsonian Magazine, Dec 2, 2010 – www.smithsonianmag.com/smart-news/tiny-islands-survived-tsunami-almost-separated-britain-europe-study-finds-180976430/

National Geographic, Resource Library, Doggerland: The Europe That Was – www.nationalgeographic.org/maps/doggerland

National Geographic Society, Continental Drift – nationalgeographic.org/encyclopedia/continental-drift/

PHYS.org, Ancient DNA from Doggerland, separates the U.K. from Europe – www.phys.org/news/2020-07-ancient-dna-doggerland-uk-europe.html

PHYS.org, Stone tool changes may show how Mesolithic hunter-gatherers responded to changing climate, July 17, 2019 – www.phys.org/news/2019-07-stone-tool-mesolithic-hunter-gatherers-climate.html

Q-Mag-org, The Great Plain of Atlantis – Was it Doggerland? – www.q-mag-org/the-great-plain-of-atlantis-was-it-in-doggerland.html

Rivera, Adam N., Scientists have discovered What These Barbed Artifacts Really Are, Ukraine Business Journal, Dec. 22, 2020 – wwwtheubj.com/science/4457/the-barbed-points/

Schulting, Rick J., Mesolithic skull cults', Research Gate, University of Oxford – www.researchgate.net/publication/275542043_Mesolithic_%27skull_cults9027

Smith, Oliver, Momber, Gary, Bates, Richard, Garwood, Paul, Fitch, Simon, Pallen, Mark, Gaffney, Vincent, Allaby, Robin G., Sedimentary DNA from a submerged site reveals wheat in the British Isles 8000 years ago, *Science New Series*, Vol. 347, No. 6225 (Feb.,2015 pp998-1001

Smithsonian Magazine, Never Heard of Doggerland? Blame Climate Change from Millenia Ago – www.smithsonian.com/science-nature/never-heard-of-doggerland-blame-climate-change-from-millenia-ago-72154423/

Spinney, Laura, Searching for Doggerland, National Geographic – www.naturalgeographic.com/magazine/2012/12/doggerland/

The Conversation, Doggerland's lost world shows

melting glaciers have drowned lands before, and may again, May 9, 2014 – www.theconversation.com/doggerlands-lost-world-shows-melting-glaciers-have-drowned-lands-before-and-may-again-26772

Wessex Archaeology, The Secrets of Doggerland – www.wessexarch.co.uk/news/secrets-doggerland

White, Mark J., Things to Do in Doggerland When You're Dead: Surviving O1S3 at the Northwestern-most Fringe of Middle Paleolithic Europe, World Archaeology, Vol. 138 No. 4, *Debate in "World Archaeology"* Dec. 2006, pp547-575

Wickham-Jones, Caroline, Living in Mesolithic Scotland, Archaeology – www.mesolithic.co.uk/blog/2019/07/03/3052-2/

Free Books by Charles River Editors

We have brand new titles available for free most days of the week. To see which of our titles are currently free, click on this link.

Discounted Books by Charles River Editors

We have titles at a discount price of just 99 cents everyday. To see which of our titles are currently 99 cents, click on this link.